IN ARDUIS AUDAX

HELEN & MICHAEL
OPPENHEIMER

# HALF ANGELS

ELISABETH MONTEFIORE

# HALF ANGELS

a book for parents
about children

THE FAITH PRESS
7 Tufton Street, London, SW 1

FIRST PUBLISHED IN 1961

© *Elisabeth Montefiore, 1961*

PRINTED IN GREAT BRITAIN
*in 11pt. Baskerville type*
BY THE FAITH PRESS LTD
LEIGHTON BUZZARD

DEDICATED TO

H.

T.

J.

C.

# CONTENTS

# 1

## INTRODUCTORY

'The lyf so short, the craft so long to lerne.'

CHAUCER

THIS is not a book about how to be a mother, or even how not to be a mother. What I know about children is a mere amalgam of childhood memories, the daily instruction administered by my own children, their friends, and the children of my friends. Help and ideas come from friends and books. Not even to amuse my family would I dare to offer public advice on the art of being a mother. Nor am I trying to indicate an ideal at which mothers should aim. In the first place admirable books for this purpose exist, in the second place I have to admit that ideals do not inspire me : they depress me. I remember the absolutely charming Vice-Principal of my husband's theological college talking to a group of ordinands' wives, all markedly alarmed by the future, and he said 'I know just the vicar's wife who ought to come and talk to you. She's good looking and delightful and well dressed, and a marvellous mother and knows the parish from A to Z.' He was, I think, mildly puzzled by our total lack of response. It is not admirable that my spirits should sink when I am exhorted to be like X who has four children, no help, copes perfectly and has never been seen to lose her temper, but sink they do, and perhaps I am not alone in this. Far more encouraging, surely, is G. K. Chesterton's splendid maxim : 'If a thing is worth doing, it is worth doing badly.' I think this feeling afflicts us chiefly in fields where we know ourselves to be incompetent or uncertain. Thus a housewife who enjoys cooking in a modest way likes to increase her skill if she can and takes pleasure in reading about the improbable masterpieces which she herself

9

will never concoct; but a housewife who dislikes and is bored by cooking will tend to feel if she's given a cookery book that she is being 'got at.' Excellence is always to be admired; it is comparisons that are odious.

As a matter of fact I would never have written this book if I had not been asked to write one on 'motherhood.'[1] I was also instructed *not* to read around the subject. In this way I was driven to consider what I admit does interest me: that is to say, what being a mother really is, what it finally involves and implies. On reading the papers and weeklies I began to notice a flow of articles suggesting that parents feel uncertain about their aims, and a flood of questions from anxious parents: How shall I control my teen-age daughter or son? How can I teach my five-year-old to be generous, to be polite, and so on and on.

It is obvious that to be a mother is to take on several jobs, some of which can be isolated and handed on to someone else if one has the money to engage a cook, a cleaner, a housemaid. If the list includes a first class, loving nanny is there anything left? Never having had a nanny, I do not know the answer to this, but I should have thought it was 'Yes.' The bearing and bringing up of children touches one's personality at its core: it is a mode of being, neither superior nor inferior to any other mode, and I have tried to consider it as such. This means that I have found myself trying to think about such matters as the nature of love, which then leads one to think both about ultimate reality and about how the human being learns to love: it has also meant trying to consider the everyday world in which we live. I may as well say at once that I carry no theological, psychological or sociological guns.

Writing this book has taught me to believe that it matters enormously that we should spare time to assess our personal

[1] I do not care for this particular word, useful though it ought to be, and have elsewhere preferred a periphrasis for it.

lives, our beliefs, our society, and that we should readily ask such questions as 'Is this true?' and 'What does this mean?' The wife of a German pastor who had been spending a year in another country recently said to me : 'You know, we are so glad to be back in England. Where we have been it is like in Germany. People are not interested in politics; they *like* believing what they are told and that is so dangerous. We have seen it in Germany. In England you still care how men in public life behave.' I thought this an extravagant compliment and still do. All the same her observation is relevant. She did not mean that more people should organize meetings and attend study groups or write to the papers. If people do these things, they do them usually because they like doing them and not necessarily because they have been thinking. She meant, rather, that to live in a cocoon of personal satisfactions is dangerous. We can put power in the hands of people unfitted to exercise it, perhaps by not bothering to vote against them. Women in general do not much take to politics, whether national or local. Politics is a game to be played wherever there is power waiting to be used ; it is on the whole a masculine obsession. Women have been pushed around for so long that they still often exercise authority with difficulty and they tend to rely on charm or terror. There are pleasing exceptions to this state of things, and I certainly do not regard female human nature as immutably given.

Frau X's comment can apply more generally. In the main, women deal with the everyday fabric of life, and what this is like depends largely on them. To be complacent is to be insensitive, and in any context this is dangerous. To be a woman is to be capable of bearing life ; to be a mother is to be responsible for a small piece of the pattern of civilization. A father shares but normally delegates this responsibility. On the whole making a home is Mum's job, as appears but too painfully when she is ill. It involves a number of skills, most of them individually easy to acquire ; it is usually necessary to operate several of these skills at once wherein lies entertainment or exasperation. The vicar calls just as one has begun to extract a rash of splinters and the surgeon-comforter becomes a sub-standard hostess as well. Late afternoon finds one cook, nanny, house-parlourmaid, chief assistant to school prep., perhaps hostess again. Altogether it would be a poor look-out for our families if women were not 'varium et semper mutabile.' Naturally this quality is not confined to housewives; it is essential to nurses, to social workers and to air hostesses to name a few. The only difference is that while her children are young there is no time or place in which a mother stops being a mother. The fact that she is comfortingly there to be shouted for at night is part of the pattern in which children live.

Again when families are very young, the year's rhythm comes to them chiefly through their mother. Through her birthdays are celebrated, Christmas cake and pudding made and stockings filled; she makes the Shrove Tuesday pancakes, the hot cross buns and the summer picnics. She makes the glowing jellies (so tasteless and so adored) while the children 'help' to ice cakes for a party. Cooking with children underfoot is not a tranquil occupation, but they love to be there and it introduces them to some of the pleasures of appreciation. Bread dough is charming to play with, baking bread has a delicious smell; there are bowls to lick and currants to steal. Food is most important to children. The convention that polite people do not discuss it seems to me ridiculous when the subject is so fascinating.[2] Real greediness is disgusting, of course, but to be high-minded about food implies surely that man considers himself superior to the physical creation. Food and the preparation of food offers a whole world of colour and texture to be explored. It is also one way in which

[2] In this country, the attitude to food is commonly less high-minded than barbarous. People can and do devour such things as steam-baked white bread, tinned 'garden' peas, potato crisps, 'cream' made of 'edible fats,' and monosodium glutamate disguised as soup. Chickens and their eggs emerge flavourless from the battery. The housewife clashing her pots and pans is here a potential guardian of civilization.

the family ethos is expressed. Most mothers love feeding their families but we do, I must admit, sometimes get fixed ideas about who likes what and the family sometimes hesitate to tell us that they are sick of ice-cream on Sundays—or whatever it is. They do greatly err; this tendency in Mums should be trampled on, and husbands can do great good by making occasional forays into the kitchen even if the results are odd. Husband and wife together (for it is *together* no matter who does the choosing and buying) create a way of living with a flavour of its own which marks their home wherever it may be.

This then is our occupation which is able to engage all our

skill of mind and heart. We practise it in a rapidly changing society, and in a world dangerous in a peculiarly baffling way; the common life of this country secures material needs perhaps but not those of the spirit. All this and much more makes family life less easy to achieve but not less important. We cannot now organize our family life and ignore the world outside, even if we would, and so we had better try as well as may be to interpret it. If one compares this task to the making of a picture, the advice, so much of it so excellent, which pours from the press could be compared to a discussion of painting techniques. People would argue about colour and line and how the paint is put on to the canvas, but they would not often discuss why a picture is painted or what principles, if any, underlie that art. Perhaps parents, like painters, must work this one out for themselves. It is what I have tried to do in the following chapters. They are of course inadequate, but in a sense inadequacy, not success, is my subject. There is no advice, good or bad, I hope; I have tried to say truthfully what I think, working from personal experience. Certainly all the stories are true, although not all have happened to me.

I am a Christian and a member of the Church of England and I have necessarily written as such. The divisions between Christians seem to me, as I suspect to many lay people, disgraceful and boring, certainly irrelevant to my present purpose. Yet I should think as I do about the care of young children even if I were not a Christian, nor should I dream of dismissing the wisdom and love which appear in the writings of non-Christians and agnostics, and can be seen in their lives. For my purpose the one true division comes between those who know that it is wrong for any reason whatever to treat any human being as a thing, and those who are not so particular. I do not need to give examples of this. It is a division which brings to light what people really believe contrasted with what they think they believe : some who do not say 'Lord, Lord' are far more sensitive in this respect than some who do.

All the same, to believe that Jesus Christ is God's Son makes a difference. Among some Christians there is a quality not to be found elsewhere. It is a different way of living. They meet calamity not with fortitude merely. If they give, it is always more than the reasonable share of time, love or money which prudence would suggest. My father, holidaying in hill country, had to have a sudden operation. In the two or three days before he died he not only uttered no complaint but lay contemplating the mercies of God. At the time I took this for granted because it was of a piece with all I had known of him. My mother has never been too busy or too tired to help people with that most valuable gift, her own time. A stream of singularly varied people came to our house, sat and talked; she would give no hint of the ironing for eight that had to be done. I can think of many others whose lives are lit by the same light, who look ordinary and are not. This they have in common, that they never feel they have done their share or cannot reasonably be asked to do more. They know that love never draws the line, never keeps accounts. They are sustained not by unusual generosity, energy or good temper but by Love Himself dwelling in them, fashioning them to his own likeness. At least this is what happens so far as I can see, but this book is not about them.

At half-term we often visit the aquarium in the Zoological Laboratory in Cambridge. Although the baby alligator is the major attraction [3] we always have a look at the axolotls. These are a kind of newt or salamander which live and propagate themselves in larval form. They are capable if removed to suitable conditions of developing into true salamanders. I have tried to explore the point at which the human spirit learns to love and therefore to develop. Most of us have to learn love twice, once as children and then, early or late, again. The axolotl has to wait for someone to move it; in our case Love does the waiting, and will not move us into light against our will.

[3] Regrettably, the shrunken heads at the anthropological museum are an even bigger draw.

15

## 2

## LOVE: DIVINE AND HUMAN

> Love seeketh not itself to please,
> Nor for itself hath any care,
> But for another gives its ease,
> And builds a heaven in Hell's despair.
>
> WILLIAM BLAKE

IT is sound nursery practice to begin at the beginning. If I am to consider the nature of my work as a mother this is less easy than it looks. I can start from my own experience: husband and children, the circumstances of everyday life, the childhood that still lives within me, the heady falling in love which does not last, the equally strong and more enduring impulse to care for and protect the family, the defeat of loneliness, the pleasures of chat. I can select and explore; one aspect of life will illuminate another but there is no explanation here, nothing which makes sense of the whole. Experience whether considered as a sequence or jumble of happenings does not explain itself.

I conclude that the beginning is not with me. How can I hope to understand the single sample of life that I am without asking who made me and why? The enquiry therefore begins at the true beginning: God.

At once there are obvious difficulties since no man has seen God at any time; but the Christian knows that God as well as constantly revealing himself in creation specially revealed himself in Jesus Christ. We can look at him and so looking can learn. We know that God is love, that he made and controls the universe and that it is his will that we shall perfectly love him. S. John tells us that we are to dwell in God and he in us, we are to live in love. What is it like? S. Paul and S. John, the mystics, the saints, some poets can help us here; yet I believe that it is important that we should try to find our own words too. They are hopelessly inadequate, but so is all human expression and God will not mind this any more than a mother is offended by the clumsiness of her small child's home-made present.

We are accustomed to think of God in his relation to us, as loving, forgiving, redeeming us and loved by us in return. Indeed, how we experience that love depends to some extent at least on the kind of person we are. Some people are burdened by the thought of sin and to them God is forgiveness. Others love him in his creation, chiefly with the mind. Others again are chiefly conscious of his loving protection. At Christmas we celebrate the birth of Christ and the year continues with reminders of what he is to us. Once a year, however, we keep a day on which God is praised for his own sake when on Trinity Sunday the Church remembers not only that God has created all things but that *for his pleasure* they are and were created. This unlimited energy of selfless joy is our inheritance. This is the true nature of love.

Such words say both too little, for they are hardly a beginning, and too much for they describe what has not been seen. Nonetheless we must use *some* words for the final reality, we need to have *some* idea what we mean by the divine Love which was before all worlds, now is, and will always be. We need in fact to remember that God does not exist in order that we may love him. Strictly speaking, we are not necessary to him, he is complete without us. This may seem a bleak notion at first but is really a most comforting one. There is a poem about a girl who longed to be loved for herself alone and not her yellow hair: if there is one being who entirely wills my good for my sake, who needs nothing that I can do in return, then I can be happy indeed thus to be unnecessary. What is more, the divine love which itself cannot be described has entered our world, been

17

B

subject to time and space, has let human life happen to it as it happens to us. If we want to know how love behaves and is treated in this world the gospels tell us in plain terms. Our Lord Jesus Christ lived for nearly thirty years in a quiet village which thought it knew all about him and was we may suppose upon the whole indifferent. Once his ministry began indifference vanished. People rushed after him and badgered him. His friends loved, trusted and misunderstood him; those who became his enemies feared and hated him. He is the revelation of divine love. Looking at him we learn that in our world such love in the end involves deprivation, suffering, rejection, but is not altered by them, much less defeated. Jesus is a commanding figure, never a pathetic one.[1] In the extremity of physical pain he yet could pray for his executioners, care for his mother, receive a repentant soul. Almost his last word is a shout of triumphant accomplishment. Love, then, even while pain and evil are at work upon it, can master them both. 'And,' says our Lord, 'if you will allow my love to invade you, I will not rest until in you also it is master.' It is both an assurance and a warning.

Let us now turn to ourselves. If we look at love as a form of instinctive human behaviour its variety is endless; yet one can on the whole observe that human love is biologically useful, that it is need seeking satisfaction, above all that it is a source of energy. Our experience of it is coloured by convention, by religion, by civilization but beneath all these is energy, neutral in itself, good or not good according to the use made of it. I think that instinctive human love has this in common with divine love: it is a source of power.

It is obvious enough that love between the sexes is not selfless in its origin. Might it not be said that the love of parents for their children is a truly selfless thing? If it is, then why should

---

[1] It is deplorable that popular religious art should so constantly endow him with weak good looks, and flowing white robes quite unsuitable for one accustomed to walk in the hills before dawn.

the desire for children be so strong? Many mothers feel in their hearts that they are most unselfish. We squander our time and talents on our families, piling their plates with food, leaping out of bed at night when they cry. The readiness with which we do this should warn us that here is not virtue but instinct, and a good thing too or the human young would seldom reach maturity. 'Unselfishness' of this kind can be a menace. Unfortunately, husbands on the whole derive no special satisfaction from seeing that their offspring eat well, may believe that a smaller share of strawberries, or bacon but no egg is a genuine deprivation to their wives, and not like to interfere with such unselfishness; or they may simply notice nothing until Mum is regularly and deliberately taking less than her share of any treat. Her husband will we hope quickly educate such a wife in the Higher Selfishness.

Where meanwhile is what most of us mean by 'love'? What are we to say of the singing voice, the ideal vision, which transforms the most ordinary young people, which triumphs over time and distance, which when we are very young seems in itself a goal? In the literature which celebrates this love the beloved is almost a religious symbol and the love itself is seen as an ennobling passion. Yet much of our love poetry is about the lover's own feelings rather than the object of his love, and what, one sometimes wonders, were the thoughts of the silent, shadowy ladies who provoked these outbursts?

At all events this rose-golden cloud is what we now expect. Marriage began as contract, and the romantic vision operated outside marriage when it first arose in the Middle Ages; later what with passionate Protestant poets, and social changes increasing the number of people with time to enjoy their emotions, romantic love came to be part of marriage:

> 'Here, Love his golden shafts employs, here lights
> His constant lamp, and waves his purple wings,
> Reigns here and revels.'

What would Milton have said of a recent serious novel which was described as an investigation of modern love 'analysing and dissecting it in a variety of manifestations, including incest, nymphomania and homosexuality by both sexes as well as normal obsessive passion'? This approach and that of the gossip columns to 'romance' seem different in kind from ideal romantic love: yet such love is not selfless in its nature as divine love is, and if it is made an end in itself it will degenerate. The greater part of mankind has never bothered with the romantic conception of love. It does not appear in the New Testament. Instead Jesus observed (and it does seem odd that these words are not part of our marriage service): 'From the beginning of creation God made them male and female. For this reason a man shall leave his father and mother and be joined to his wife, and the two shall become one. So they are no longer two but one.' It can, I think, be maintained that falling in love is less love itself than the prelude to love. A young woman newly engaged knows herself to be much 'in love' and can hardly believe that the comfortable middle-aged housewife sitting next to her in the bus has ever loved as she does. Yet, seen from within marriage, courtship seems singularly threadbare. One feels now that true love began with marriage, is nourished by knowledge rather than by illusion, and is most deeply personal in its physical expression. Married love can glow with the divine self giving : husband and wife have committed their lives to each other; they put aside shyness and reserve because these have no place in love's expression; they bring to each other all that they are and all that they are to become. They spend the 'sweet hours . . . that put the spirit in the body's debt' and as time passes learn to know each other's mind and nature, to be content that their partner shall know their fears and follies. I am writing as a mother and do not wish to say much of marriage, that bond at once so public and so intensely private; but it cannot be too strongly affirmed that the loving trust of husband and wife in each other is the rock on which the security of their children is founded.

Marriage is one among many human activities in all of which divine love can operate whether it is recognized as such or not. It is a beginning only, not an end. God wills that we should become such as he is : marriage and parenthood are two of the means whereby he can refashion our human affections into the love 'which seeketh not itself to please.' To be married, then, is not 'better' than to be single, nor is it 'better' to be celibate than married. We are all to learn the same lesson but in different kinds of school. Nothing matters except present obedience to God's will, which for a mother may mean that she stops talking in order to watch the traffic, or does that awful mending, or says her prayers.

# 3

## LOVE AND THE BABY

'Friday's child is loving and giving.'

W H E N parents think about the qualities they want to see in their children, the odds are that a loving heart comes high on the list. The preceding chapter is concerned with what love essentially is, this one with how the human being learns to love. We know [1] that the first infant years are overwhelmingly important in this respect. Since it is not easy to translate knowledge into understanding it may be worth while to consider the matter a little further.

A new-born baby's world is his mother. At first he receives from her food, warmth and comfort. Quickly she becomes the source of his pleasure and security as well. All that is good from a baby's point of view, even his experience of life itself, is mediated through her. Hers is the breast at which he gulps, hers the hands which count his toes, caress his body, hold him safe in his delicious splashy bath and, less desirably, soap him. (A remarkable parson instructed me : 'The thing to do is to get hold of an isthmus; then the creature *can't* slip off your knee.') A baby's mother sings to him, talks nonsense to him, rocks him. Other people look after him too but none so consistently as she. She introduces him to his five senses. An adult, blind from birth, was cured of his blindness but could at first only 'see' an object by touching it. He had to learn the connection between each visual image and the knowledge conveyed by his sense of touch. How hard our children work even from the first ! It is fascinating to watch a crawling baby learning his world, always at first via

---

[1] Any who doubt if we do know this might read *Child Care and the Growth of Love* by John Bowlby or *The Origins of Love and Hate* by Ian Suttie, Pelican books.

his mouth. Rusks, toys, bits of coal, in they all go. Not that life is all a giddy round of pleasure. Babies learn to their disgust that other wills conflict with theirs, the nice piece of coal is taken away, social occasions are rudely interrupted by nonsense about time for sleep. A sympathetic five-year-old observed : 'I do think Baby has an awful life, Mummy.'

He grows and thrives partly because of sensible physical care, partly because he is loved and secure. Although he soon learns to enjoy the company of his father and any older brothers or sisters there may be, he depends chiefly on one person. He cannot learn all that he needs to learn without the abiding security which is derived from a single reliable source. This is the reason why babies in institutions develop less quickly than those in normal homes. They do not belong to any one nurse, nurses have regular hours on and off, they may take a holiday or change their job. Babies who suffer many changes of care in the first year of life may grow up without the power to feel affection. A mother's love is thus a kind of food developing the child as a whole person.[2]

A mother teaches her child to love by pouring love upon him. Thus loved and secure he first enjoys the satisfaction of a possessive love ; later comes the wish to please, later again comes willingness to put personal wants aside for the sake of another. It is a remarkable process if one reflects upon it, and unnerving : for while relatively few men are priests, the humblest, most ignorant mother mediates God to her infant children. She is his vice-reine. We may be thankful for the instincts which cause us to be all this without our giving the matter a thought.

It is conventional at Christmas to think of Jesus as poor and cold, one of the dispossessed. This is sentimental. He had all the riches that any human baby needs. Mary was there to keep him

---

[2] Is it not akin to the spiritual food given to us at the Eucharist?

warm, fed and adored, Joseph to protect. He had a settled home. His foster father was not a labourer hired by the day but an artisan, who even had some property in Bethlehem. Every one in the village knew, or thought they knew, who he was. In other words he was born into security, though of a modest kind.[3] There were plenty of the dispossessed in the land of Christ's birth. There were many orphans and slaves but the Son of God was not born among them. Must we not conclude that the need of the developing human personality for security of this kind is absolute? People do triumph over a deprived childhood but the scars they carry are permanent, and often such deprivation is the cause of the miseries of neurosis, if not of the affectionless character which ends up in conflict with Law. Our Lord's humanity was flawless and teaches us to take the needs of all children seriously.[4]

Although this need for security diminishes and becomes less

[3] So we need not feel guilty about the Christmas feast. Xmas is perhaps different.
[4] In the Church of England we are often shy of our Lady; but if we believe that Jesus Christ was fully human, and that environment is important to the growing child, how can we fail to love and honour the mother who looked after him during the hidden years?

concentrated upon the mother, it remains immensely important in children well past the infant stage. It is easy to inflict injuries by our mistakes. Thus, because it was the only way to manage a necessary holiday we placed our first toddler in an excellent baby home. We telephoned the home regularly and all was well. At the end of the week we collected her and I hardly recognized her. Just one week. Even schoolchildren look for their mother when they come home. The presence of their parents somewhere in the house brings a sense of well-being to younger children who then settle down to tea and prep. with contented humming noises. Naturally this situation has its dangers. Parents and children can devour each other. Instinctive love is necessary but its effects are good or bad according to the will that exercises it. Our children are safe with us only if our natural love has become at least partly selfless; without us they are not safe at all.

Here we meet a difficulty related to our present high standard of living. The emphasis on expensive material possessions exerts pressure on women to continue paid work after marriage, even while the children are still babies or well under three years old. Some mothers can command such salaries as enable them to employ full-time nannies. Other mothers rely on helps and nursery schools of varying competence. A conscientious mother can feel that she has arranged for her child to be properly looked after and that she is also able to give him absolutely everything she wants him to have. We have seen that a very young child does not need or want luxuries and that his security will be centred upon one person. The conclusion is obvious. A mother who wishes to work outside the home while her baby is under two has an absolute duty to provide a genuine substitute for herself. I think the situation is different for a mother who, because her husband is ill or has died, *must* work outside the home. Children understand however inarticulately the difference between: 'I can't be with you' when this is true and when it means 'I don't really want to be with you.' Nor is it surprising

if the child's love goes to his substitute-mother. It seems possible
that reserve and lack of ease in personal relationships and all the
stiff upper lip nonsense is due in large measure to the banish-
ment of children from the company of their parents. Therefore,
although mothers may curse, and life while the children are very
young is often a weariness of the flesh, the work of caring for
them is incomparably important.

Housewives often feel that their work is humdrum because
there are so many of them doing it. One's old school may possibly be more impressed by the pupil who is now Deputy

Assistant Director at the Circumlocution Office than by the one who is Mum to a riotous family. This is merely due to the human tendency to value most what is scarce and to take for granted, if not to despise, what is common or abundant. We all want to be special privileged people. Exclusiveness is but one of the forms of pride and has nothing to do with God, the creator of abundance. Light sparkles on water for all to see, bluebells and primroses fill woods and hedges in millions, who can count the stars? Love too is common. 'Only God can be had for the asking, only Heaven is given away.' Fathers and mothers are allowed to share in this. The creation of a baby is the work of our bodies : into our hands is also put authority to govern, in the early years, the growth in body, mind and spirit of that baby.

Very young children appear to live almost wholly in physical terms. A baby spends its time eating and sleeping with a little sociability thrown in. In fact, however, children live on two levels at once so that physical actions become the vehicle of such spiritual states as love, ill-temper, anxiety or even carelessness. If my baby being hungry cries and is fed, he experiences both the satisfaction of hunger and my willingness to give him that satisfaction. If he is sick in his cot and howls with discomfort so that I come to clear up the nasty mess and comfort him, he has learned, subconsciously, that the universe is orderly and that I care to restore his peace. Years ago, I was at a tea-party with a young mother who believed strongly in time-tables. For half an hour we listened to the yells of her near-by infant who had indeed been sick as his mother discovered when it was 'time' to pick him up. What did this child learn? That his discomfort would remain until some quite arbitrary decree was relaxed. We may be thankful that rigid time-tables for babies are out of fashion. They do no harm to the placid child, but can certainly harm the sensitive. As time passes we may have occasion to remind our family that life is unfair, but their first knowledge of the created universe should be that it is good, as they learn from us to trust, to love and to give.

# 4

## LOVE AND THE GROWING CHILD

A child that prospers, carries everywhere
A little dome of pleasant secret air.
We who receive his unconcerned embrace
Perceive it sacred, round the soft-nosed face.

FRANCES CORNFORD

I ASKED our children what kind of things they thought a mother should do. The eldest (thirteen) was in no doubt and rattled off:

Bring them up to be true Christian children;

teach them to be courteous;

give them lots of good food to make them grow.

Later I asked what they thought fathers were for and received a clear amused reply:

To earn money to feed their poor starving children;

protection;

someone for Mummy to confide in when her children are too overpowering.

What interested me was that the younger children were not sufficiently detached to have immediate ideas to express, and that as parents we were firmly assigned our traditional roles. How much or how little a father takes part in the actual bringing up of his children depends largely on his temperament and circumstances. In general he plays a far greater part than he did; some fathers, particularly among the clergy (who work from home) do a great deal. All the same I am sure that it is important first that child care, like the kitchen, should remain chiefly the mother's department, and secondly, that the father should represent authority, protection and safety. Since he is out

all day earning the family's keep, a father can have a marvellously helpful detachment, and may be better able than his harassed wife to see just where things have gone wrong. I imagine that if he is much in the hurly-burly himself then his detachment is likely to be impaired.

One might add that a father represents fun. He has scarcity value, he tends to be relaxed and fairly uninhibited with his children because for him they are 'time-off.' They love it. Some fathers will even cope with babies, I have seen one washing the nappies with a book propped up in front of him; some prefer their offspring at a distance until they are conversable. I do not think it possible to define fatherly activity in any but general terms.

As a mother and father mull things over together what should

30

be their aims? One thing is certain: there are very few hard and fast rules. Fashions in child care change markedly, especially when it comes to food and discipline. What suits one child does not necessarily suit the next, so that parents have to discover their own family pattern, and in this matter their children will teach them a good deal. As far as practical methods are concerned there is an enormous quantity of excellent advice to be had from books and magazines, together with all manner of bright ideas, such as the delightful notion that one might hang balloons above a sick child's bed so that languid little hands could pat them to and fro. Common sense and imagination will take us a long way, and since running a home consists of making incessant small decisions requiring either or both, we might be tempted to think that we need no more. We would be wrong. No one can win a battle, build a house or make a garden without considering first what is to be achieved, and then the means to be used. So it is with children. What are their deepest needs as they move out of their prams into push-chairs, tricycles and bicycles? Among many we may select two, security and order, and perhaps a third, wonder.

Security: we have seen that a baby's security depends on his mother's devoted attention. As he grows the faithful love of his parents is the safe harbour from which he can adventure. Even when we have children of our own we look instinctively to our own parents for sympathy and interest in something of the way in which we once brought them our sea-shells or grazed knees. A mother gives physical expression to her loving care in a most characteristic gesture, folding the child in her arms. It expresses her reassurance and the child's trustfulness. Jesus took the children up into his arms and blessed them. Centuries ago when a man took an oath of loyalty, his lord, accepting it, embraced him. So lovers too, meeting or parting, hold one another. A secure child hugs us back cheerfully and wriggles off. A small child who has been hurt needs a cuddle as well as antiseptics. How admirable was my 'mother's help' who on such an occasion asked : 'Will you have it cleaned up first or have a love first?'

A second strand in security is freedom. We are ready to express our love, we are willing also to refrain from expressing it; for if we insist on such expression because that is how we feel, we are approaching possessiveness and smothering rather than mothering. Much the same applies if we allow our interest in our children to become absorption, so that we brood over them, breaking off our conversation to let them speak. The result tends to be either a self-conscious child immensely tedious to visitors, or an anxious, uneasy one. If we must so restrain our impulse, and not take too much to heart that preoccupied withdrawal, this is one of love's sacrifices. We may say perhaps that a child must know his parents love him, but must not be burdened by that knowledge. It ought to go without saying, but perhaps does not, that we do not *demand* gratitude and responsiveness from our children.

Thirdly, a child's security depends on his being accepted just as he is. Most of us can readily survive the embarrassments caused by babies and as yet un-house-trained toddlers. It is less easy not to mind if my child gets over-excited and shows off in company, or whines, or bullies children smaller than himself or is not the sort of child one might have ordered. People are sometimes keenly disappointed to have no son, or no daughter; they would prefer children less rowdy or more spirited, cleverer or less bookish, bolder or less foolhardy. They look perhaps at their shy, grubby little thumbsucker and think of the bright-eyed apple-cheeked extrovert next door whom all the local mums approve. Closer acquaintance with one such extrovert taught me that this appearance of competent good-nature was the gloss on

selfishness. Some children are transparently loving or plainly in need of help, others are perfectly charming to meet and the charm is as unreliable an index to their true selves as adult charm. We so want our children to be attractive and successful that we sometimes find it hard to support them and believe in them without qualification. A sensitive child who starts being tiresome needs more loving not less. What adult can long endure a situation in which he is continually criticized and nobody believes in him? We all know people who are insecure because at the deepest level they feel unaccepted by their parents. They commonly suffer neurosis, mild or severe, struggling all their lives against the pain of that rejection.

Even when there is no question that we love our children it is terribly easy to cause anxiety in the childish mind. Probably the best safeguard against doing this is the deliberate effort *to see each situation as it may be appearing to the child*, bearing in

33

mind the fact that a child can only judge the attitude of people towards him by their actions. An incident which started as a classic example of How Not to Do It taught me much. When our No. 1 was nearly two, No. 2 was born and was fed upstairs and all was happiness and peace. In due course No. 2 was ready for ordinary food and began to have meals with the rest of us in her high-chair. At the same time No. 1 started to create at meal-times. Being new to the job, I thought 'This is it. I will *not* be bullied by my offspring,' and for a day or two life was a trial for all. Then my husband suggested that it might have something to do with No. 2, and at last I saw : poor little No. 1, queening it alone with a foreign girl and me, now sat alone while both grown-ups concentrated on pushing food into the baby's mouth. This was an easy situation to remedy as the baby was only too happy to be left alone plastering face and hair with food while No. 1 had some attention again. It all seems so obvious now ; how simple to spot other people's mistakes, or one's own when they are long past, how anything but simple at the time ! An experienced mother will not make the mistake I have instanced, but she may hear herself saying to older children 'Stop it or . . .' and 'You really are old enough to be more sensible.' The sole agent of a child's security is faithful vigilant love.

In this connection I would like to quote from a biography [1] I happened to be reading while I was writing this book. The subject of the biography, Geoffrey Pyke, was an odd, brilliantly clever man with ideas about children which were most unconventional in the twenties. He 'used to say that the principle we should follow is to treat every child as a distinguished foreign visitor who knows little or nothing of our language or customs. If we invited a distinguished visitor to tea and he spilled his cup on the best table-cloth or consumed more than his share of cake, we should not upbraid him and send him out of the room. We should hasten to assure him that all was well. One rude remark

[1] *Pyke: The Unknown Genius,* David Lampe.

from the host would drive the visitor from the room, never to be seen again. But we address children constantly in the rudest fashion and yet expect them to behave as models of politeness.'

Second to security is order. By this I do not mean routine, though on the whole young children much prefer life to be fairly predictable. I mean that their happiness partly stems from knowing that someone else is in charge, even that they are not going to get away with misdemeanours. Our children were particularly fond of one of the foreign girls who in turn prop up our home, and we asked why. 'Because she can make us do what she wants' was the unanimous reply. The to spank or not to spank issue is irrelevant here. I think myself that Shaw was right in holding that if you beat your child you should be sure you do it in anger. It relieves irritation but is sadly subject to the law of diminishing returns and is impossible nowadays with older children, whatever may have been the case in the days of 'spare the rod and spoil the child.' All the same there are occasions when one will or the other must prevail.

At this point, one needs to distinguish inconvenient conduct from serious disobedience. The four-year-old who cut squares off the new nursery curtains to decorate his pyjama buttons was less naughty than ingenious; the seven-year-old who lightly sprinkled beds and carpets with Christmas glitter had a wonderful idea. Nor is it reasonable to expect the average child to be *interested* in being tidy or clean. Sooner or later however most of us meet a disagreeable kind of disobedience about which something has to be done. Easily the most dismal meal I have sat through was when our children consumed bread and water while the rest of us had stew; but the effect was admirable and astonishing. There was no resentment and the incident has since formed part of family folklore. Children appreciate justice and mind injustice very much indeed, including broken promises which are an aspect of injustice. They understand a punishment that fits the crime or that causes them personal inconvenience. It is probably unlikely that they will think our views reasonable since they do not work from our premises, but in their hearts they will prefer to know that there are things they may not do, for so they are safe in a world unpredictable and unsafe.

There is one other aspect of order. A five-year-old said to her mother at bed-time : 'Let's count up everybody. You one, T. two, me three. No. Let's start again. Daddy one, you two, T. three, me four, baby five.' Again, a seven-year-old discussing names said : 'Gillian Mary—she's in my family,' not 'she's my sister.' The first child tried to sort out her world, starting with the people most important to her emotionally, got in a muddle, and began again at the beginning, placing her family in a hierarchy. The second child thought of her family as something organic to which individuals belonged. Both were concerned with order.

Finally, wonder. A young child lives in a world in which things happen for the first time. It is therefore a remarkable place, and it is a long time before a baby, for instance, gets bored with the force of gravity if a handy adult will pick up what he throws out of his pram. Every May brings a miracle of dande-lions and buttercups, every autumn, conkers, and every winter, snow. Some people are astonished by the physical creation all their lives. By them nothing is taken for granted, but also nothing is a surprise because everything is remarkable. Like the White Queen they can easily believe six impossible things before break-fast. Other children, however, quickly discover that grass is always green, stone hard and that grown-ups make plans and are put out if they miscarry. Perhaps they bring in a feather and are told 'That's only a hen's feather, darling, and not very clean,' or I say 'Very nice, darling' without even looking. They could end up sure that the world they live in is easily known, and not, *in itself*, interesting. We, who know that this is not true, can foster their sense of wonder.

I do not mean that children who dislike stories of marvellous or magical events should be plagued with them. For one thing, the essence of magic is not wonder. I mean rather that we can teach them to look closely at the visible world and make discoveries. School is usually a marvellous help in all this. Young children really do not think that their parents know much about anything, unless they have proof to the contrary, whereas the lightest word of their teachers is an oracle. We cannot always down tools to 'Come and look' or be unfailingly interested, nor is this necessary unless we wish to make our little dears complete tyrants. Nevertheless we do them a service by sharing what interests us with them, if they like, and by responding to their enthusiasm. For the matter is important. 'The heavens declare the glory of God and the firmament sheweth his handiwork,' so that he who is truly fascinated by any aspect of creation, whatever his personal beliefs or character may be, thereby renders himself in some degree accessible to God.

# 5

# THE WORLD ABOUT US

'Now as I said, the way to the Celestial City lies
just through this town where this lusty fair is kept;
and he that will go to the city, and yet not go through
this town, must needs go out of the world.'

JOHN BUNYAN

WHAT has been written so far is an effort to discover to some
extent what is important in the work of a mother and in particular what are some of the emotional and spiritual needs in
children which parents exist to satisfy. The exercise is a sobering
one, yet though surely essential, it is no more than an exercise.
Actual everyday life is lived on several levels at once and sparkles
with absurdity and fun. God is not like the fussy housewife who
says 'Now this is what I want done, and, remember, there are
only two ways of doing a thing: a right way and a wrong way.'
I fancy he more resembles someone saying 'Yes, well there you
are. Get on with it and do your best.' Part of doing one's best
consists in understanding the job to be done, and also the circumstances in which it must be done. To a few of these circumstances
we now turn.

We in this country are constantly told either to rejoice over
or to beware of our present high standard of living. Never, we
hear, have so many people been so prosperous or so uninterested
in anything but their own prosperity. It may be so; yet although
Christians have long been warned against the world and Vanity
Fair they have mostly not ceased through the centuries to attend
to their own comfort before anything else. The situation is probably not new at all except in one thing: the industrial West has
discovered how to make machines do the work formerly done

by human muscle and has made possible the end of drudgery. A marked feature of our life is its dependence on gadgets like refrigerators, vacuum cleaners, washing machines, sewing machines, all admirable and all expensive. At this point nostalgic voices say: 'Yes but this so-called high standard of living has no quality. It cannot compare with life before 1914. Why, quite modest professional people could then enjoy a degree of comfort which is now only possible for the very wealthy.' This, if we are honest, is true. What bliss to come home to a meal for which one has not had to do the shopping, which one has not prepared and which one will not have to wash up; to leave untidiness which other hands will set in order, to enjoy fires which others will stoke; in fact to live a life in which *someone else does the work*. Nostalgia forgets the other half of the equation which social historians supply: our grandparents, even our parents, could live like this because millions of their fellow countrymen were not properly paid. We ourselves can live like this if we go to countries where, again, millions of people live in conditions which amount to slavery. It is surely a very good thing that in this country girls do not now have to be servants unless they so wish, and one might expect Christians to be delighted about it. Instead they often write sadly of the debasing effect of materialism upon simple people, by which they mean that the normal human being will do things the easy way if he gets half a chance but toil would be better for his soul. 'Simple people' observe the standards which their 'betters' adopt for themselves and adopt them too. Should we mind?

There is as we know only too well a less happy side to all this. The high standard of living is strictly for those who can afford it. Household equipment of all kinds is exceedingly expensive. It used to be said, untruly, that two could live as cheaply as one. The expression has almost altogether disappeared, so expensive has setting up even a modest home become. People who when single were used to having money for pleasant clothes and holi-

days discover that marriage on one person's income with a child
or two thrown in is a grind; there is for them no money for
theatres or books let alone holidays abroad, and their unencum-
bered friends rub salt in by entertaining them at length with
accounts of Glyndebourne and the Dalmatian coast. There is
thus tremendous pressure on wives to continue working when
they first marry, and to resume work as soon as possible when
the children have arrived, if a high standard of living is to be
maintained. It seems perfectly reasonable for women to go on

working until their family starts, though this can be a strain. When children are much older it is often good for everybody if Mum finds a new occupation. But when children are under five the matter is different, and this pressure to earn more money in order to buy what advertisements call 'the good things of life' may be in direct conflict with the children's need for their mother's comforting presence. The difficulty is even more acute if people have married, as they do, on the basis of their joint incomes. An unexpected baby, an illness or change of work can shake the foundation of their marriage. It is just here that the popular tradition of romantic love is less than helpful; after all prudence is said to be one of the cardinal virtues, that is, it makes possible other virtues. Courses of sermons or lectures on 'Personal relationships' are always popular. How often do they discuss the £. s. d. of love?

A second pressure on parents trying to create a home comes from the forces tending to isolate the family. The small town with a stable community is giving way to 'residential areas' where people live in housing estates and work outside them. When I was little we moved to such a small town. I do not idealize it : there was a cathedral, and quite a strongly marked social hierarchy with families which had lived there for several generations. The clergy wives did not always think it necessary to call upon Nonconformists living in the shadow of the cathedral and the slum dwellers across the road approached the precincts but once a year when gaunt, terrifying women swirled into the Deanery drive for the annual Jumble Sale. We lived at rather the wrong end of the town near the workhouse and the tramps.[1] Even so it was an easy walk through the allotments with their charming pigs into the stubble fields where we picked up partridge feathers. It was an interesting world for children, now almost lost in a chaos of new houses and traffic. Suburbs with

[1] It was during the depression when street singers were a commonplace. I remember my father sending one of us out to a man who was singing the Londonderry Air.

wide roads and nice semi-detached houses, acres of them, and
suitable spring-flowering trees are not at all the same thing. If,
as often happens, young marrieds have moved with the husband's work away from their home town, loneliness can be
extreme. Only a few people can afford to live in districts which
have character. Home, more and more, needs to be a major
source of flavour and interest until we have learned how to make
these arid districts fruitful to the mind.

A third very obvious force affecting us is the standardizing of
everyday life. We see the same papers, the same television
programmes, the same films; we buy the same tinned and
packeted foods and wear the same clothes from the same admirable chain store. None of this is in itself specially sinister or inter-
feres with our individuality. One may as well make use of mass-
production. Besides if the children badger me to buy a special
ventriloquial cereal because of the whizzo space-gadget inside it

and I refuse, I merely implant in them a strong urge to have that cereal. If I buy the cereal once in a way they discover for themselves that the space-gadget is one more boring bit of plastic and the cereal hangs around uneaten, a fact which is duly filed for reference by Mamma. So too, if parents refuse to buy comics for their children, they will read them at a friend's house just the same, for like the rest of us children are omnivorous and enjoy the second-rate as well as the good. (People often express scorn of the popular press, but away from home they nobble the Daily —, every time.) More serious are such things as the pressures of advertising and the lies that politicians tell. Children do tend to believe what they see in print, and we do not wish them to become the kind of people who disbelieve on principle every-thing they are told. It is often the case that people say a thing because they are frightened, or anxious, or proud, or want to sell us something. We may therefore be tempted to teach our children the fatally easy phrase: 'You say that because . . .' when we help them far more if we teach them to ask 'Is it true?', and to look for evidence. A second string to our bow is comedy. We can guy the strip advertisements, sing them as opera or even use psalm tunes on them. Psalm tunes are infinitely adaptable and may be tried on the social column or simple family abuse. I don't think this is irreverent, and its by-product is a livelier singing of the psalms on Sunday.

Other things are less bearable. Our lovely country-side is being quickly destroyed. We have put power to do this into the hands of men who have learned to ignore if not to dislike beautiful things. We all connive at the daily killing and injuring of our brothers and sisters on the roads. We herd the image of God twice a day on to trains packed to suffocation point. We spend a fantastic amount on alcohol, tobacco and gambling and nuclear weapons, while we still pack schoolchildren into classes of forty and more. One might add the high rate of divorce to the list. 'My people love to have it so. And what will ye do in the end thereof?'

So thinking, I sometimes despair. We cannot ignore these things; we can perhaps remember that they press upon us rather than upon our children. For the purpose of this enquiry they rank as facts rather than as evils. As a citizen I should protest against the evil, as a parent I must teach my children to be careful in road traffic. The world has always been a dangerous place, but the dangers alter their character from time to time. Young children, even children well on in school, are still in a sense in the womb. They grow there, preparing to live in the world outside, helped by us through the difficult transition to adult life. Until that time, if all is well, the exterior world does not concern them deeply. That is why reading newspapers [2] does children relatively little harm. For them divorcing film-stars are one thing, real life another. Their deepest assumption is that their home should be stable and they will quite possibly not even notice that the marriage next door has been breaking-up for months. When faced with such a fact a child's response is likely to be: 'But they've broken their promises.' This quality, this knowledge without experience, we call innocence. With it go the single-mindedness and clear sight so characteristic of children. Even when they have entered puberty and have also long been acquainted with anger, greed, jealousy and their like, children mostly have about them an immense innocence; but watching them at parties we see on some faces a sharpness, an ugly shadow. Innocence must become experience if there is to be understanding, and the shadow on these young faces is ugly because it comes from false knowledge rather than true. It is the shadow cast by such things as indulged selfishness, snobbishness [3] and an attitude towards sex which regards it as dirty. These are commonplaces of school life but need not affect a child unless they are com-

---

[2] I am thinking of reasonably responsible newspapers, not of the specialists in 'cheesecake.'

[3] Our national vice would be funny if it were not so revolting. A Christian can have the melancholy distinction of belonging to a club which would exclude Jesus of Nazareth because he was a Jew; devout Christians can be seen to feel that people out of a different, 'lower,' social box are less 'real' than their personal acquaintances.

monplaces of home life, or unless the child is unhappy or disturbed.

We live among looming terrors, and have almost become accustomed to them, yet we have moments of dread for our children. Perhaps we forget the strength and pressure of individuality. The human spirit has the power of all growing things. Roots look fragile but given time they will break concrete. God who breathed life into his creation, breathed into it also the power of renewal, and it still is his. We remember this and turn to our everyday life which looks so commonplace but is not. We may have to meet the equivalent of dragons and goblins. Children expect this: given a secure home they can be extraordinarily tough. Plenty of people live in the jungle already. The woman who comes to clean may have thieving neighbours; the plants she tries to grow will be spoiled by malice or patrolling cats. When trouble comes, as it often does, she feels no outrage. She has never expected life to be secure, but that does not stop her from putting in more plants, planning small treats for the family and showing practical kindness to the sordid and pathetic old age pensioners opposite. She lives in the present moment. It is a sound way to deal with anxiety and fear. We may have to face these squarely at times when some particular distress is upon us, but to brood over vague fears of events which we cannot control merely increases the fears and lessens courage. S. Paul when he recommended the Christians of Philippi to have in mind things that were true, honest, lovely, and worthy of praise, was not being pious but immensely practical.

In general exhilaration far exceeds fear. Our present world if unpredictable is at least not boring. To be a parent now is not a matter of routine or convention. It is not only to engage in an absorbing art, but also, along with the poets and artists, to renew the springs of our common life.

# 6

## GOD IN OUR LIVES

O Lux beatissima, reple cordis intima
Tuorum fidelium. Sine tuo numine
Nihil est in homine, nihil est innoxium.

*The Golden Sequence*

IT is perhaps not too difficult to see and approve the things we
ought to do; faithfully to perform them is another matter
altogether. I do not myself think that one can get anywhere at
all without firstly a reasonably coherent belief about the point
and purpose of life and secondly some power to act on that
belief. If either of these is mine it feels less like an achievement
than a gift.

Women are sometimes said to be religious by nature; it is
probably truer to say that many of them discover quite early
that they need help. Basically this is due to fear. Even in this
country a girl who hitch-hikes alone is asking for trouble; in
some districts she is wise not even to glance across the road when
she goes home at night; many of us can remember the footsteps
that came up from behind in the days of the blackout, and even
though they belonged to nice, civil soldiers it was a disagreeable
experience. I think that for some of us this fear is reinforced by
fear of the dark. (I was once immensely comforted to learn that
this can afflict men too.) A mother has faced something more.
Having a baby is now, in countries like ours, more agreeable as
well as far safer than it has ever been before. Indeed, where all
is normal many women find it a satisfying and creative process.
All the same, even an experienced mother of several children
can know an occasional twinge of nameless panic. It is not birth
itself one fears, but isolation and the strange process which has

taken command of one's body. The new baby has been described as a treasure lying at the end of a dark valley; his mother must go down through the valley to fetch it, and she must go alone. Such panic is fleeting and can be subdued by fortitude, but it sufficiently prevents one from feeling master of one's fate. Jesus, who steadfastly set his face towards Jerusalem, allows us to know the faint shadow of that resolution, when, by our will, something beyond our control quickens and grows within us. God owed his humanity to the girl who said : 'Be it unto me according to thy word.'

Women have always been attracted by our Lord. In his earthly life he must have staggered them for he treated them as people and friends. (S. John records that his disciples marvelled that he was talking with a woman.) Even now in our society it is fairly unusual for a woman to feel that she herself is as noticeable as her sex. (Men and women in religious orders are often particularly good company because people are people to them rather than objects of sex.) The gospels are full of stories about women, beginning with the Mother of God, and very vivid they are. The women are usually a nuisance : importunate like the Syro-Phœnician woman, ruining dinner parties with their embarrassing alabaster boxes, fussing horribly like poor Martha, timid yet persistent, like the woman who touched Jesus' garment in the crowd. Women stood beside the cross of Jesus until he died,[1] and a woman who had been (as people used so oddly to say) 'no better than she ought to be' was the first person to see the Risen Lord. He still exerts a powerful attraction, but it has to be admitted that our response is often not much better than a sentimental, wistful affection directed to his earthly person.

Jesus had at least two stern words for women. On one occasion

---

[1] We are sometimes told that S. John took our Lady away that she might be spared her Son's last agony. No mother will believe this. She had thrown in her lot with a convicted blasphemer and by so doing had cut herself off from her family. S. John therefore 'took her to his home.'

there was an emotional gush: 'Blessed is the womb that bare thee.' It received the sharp retort: 'Blessed rather are those who hear the word of God and keep it!' Later when he was carrying his cross he turned to the wailing women who were so sorry for him and said: 'Daughters of Jerusalem, do not weep for me, but weep for yourselves and for your children. For behold the days are coming when they will say "Blessed are the barren."' To use our Lord as a source of comfort, merely to gaze at him with emotion will not do. Our need of security, our awakened affection are merely starting-points: we are to learn to do his will. To be a Christian is to be offered power to choose the good and refuse the evil, power to become holy, power to be what we

are meant to be, power to love. All other activity is secondary
to this: we cannot love those dearest to us safely unless we love
God first. This is perhaps an unpalatable idea because it sounds
as though I am being asked to love someone better than I love
my husband and my children. In a sense the demand is exactly
this, but the someone is God, he who is the source of being,
holiness and love.

What, in everyday terms, does all this mean? Thousands of us
are baptized, even communicant, Christians and know very well
that this consciousness of power, of growth in goodness, is not
conspicuous in our lives, although we quite often meet it in other
people. Here I can write only from what I have known. Religious
experience is as varied as the individuals in whom it operates, so
that what helps one person is useless to another. It is, however,
I think, true that the busy mother of children faces peculiar
difficulties if she seriously considers trying to live the Christian
life.

Christians believe that their daily life depends for its quality
on the inner life, and that this inner life is nourished by three
things: prayer, public worship (above all the Holy Communion)
and brooding upon the word of God in Holy Scripture.
Obviously, no one knows how other Christians get along, but I
am fairly sure that many of us neither pray nor read our Bibles
effectively. The housewife is at some disadvantage here: for
prayer, real prayer, requires ordered concentration and the same
is true of Bible study. But the essence of housekeeping is interruption—by husband, by children, by the milkman, by the
telephone, by the man who wants to read the gas meter, or
deliver coal or sell brushes and polish. The clergy are summoned
to God's house by a bell rung always at the same time; however
busy the rest of their day, their time for prayer is rightly secure.
No one could possibly blame them for not wholly understanding
this particular difficulty. In fact many of them do understand,

49

D

and one once admitted to me that he rather assumed that a busy housewife could not be expected to say her prayers; but I have yet to hear a talk on prayer, addressed even to mothers of very young children, which offers anything except the classical pattern. Thus every Lent women embark on patterns of prayer suitable to theological students and perhaps keep going until the next family illness.

We are often told to pray; we are even more often urged to use the sacraments; it is less often suggested that to read and brood over the Gospels is as necessary for spiritual nourishment as formal prayer. Yet I have found for myself that this is so. There must be quite a number of people who have learned to think that to avail oneself of the Church's sacraments is all that matters. It is perfectly true that they are a marvellous sheet anchor, as well as a constant gentle reminder of him who waits; but they are not magic and will not make us holy by themselves. A time comes when something causes us to examine our inner life carefully and we see that it is barely smouldering ashes. Then a book or some apparently casual remark shows us what is wrong, and now we feel helpless indeed. For nothing is harder than to impose a regular habit of time spent apart with God on the kind of life a housewife leads, not because there is no time but because as we have seen she can never be certain that any one part of the day will be free of interruption. 'Get up early' she is sometimes told, and so no doubt she should. But we are thinking of an undisciplined person who has not got much further than feeling that she is going the wrong way about things. To urge her to do what she knows already she ought to be doing but somehow cannot is not much help. Besides, I sometimes think that more allowance might be made for the physical hard work a housewife undertakes. Not only is she often up at night when the children are small, but in effect she spends her day shifting weights. Has any one tried calculating just how many pounds she has lifted by the time she has brought home the shopping, cooked, and attended to her children? Any woman who has worked before her marriage, and worked hard, knows that looking after a home and children is vastly more taxing physically than anything except other manual labour.

At one time I told myself that one could get on perfectly well by means of arrow prayers, or prayers said while one peeled the potatoes or ironed or waited for the bus. But the terrible thing is that those who insist that we *must* read the Gospels and spend time quietly in the presence of God are perfectly right. How can we grow like him unless we feed our minds upon him? How can we know his voice unless we listen for it? How can we learn to love unless we wait upon love itself? Our earthly friendships must be kept in repair if they are to prosper; Jesus said 'I have called you friends.' How then are we to attempt what seems so impossible? Or do we resign ourselves to being second-class Christians? Not willingly, for our life as wives and mothers requires us to love truly and to learn this we need to dwell with God.

None of what is written here applies to the disciplined woman who has early learned the ways that lead to life; and no one way of interior life will do for everybody. But I think it likely that there are some who genuinely find rules difficult and who, truly longing to learn to love our Lord, are harrowed and appalled each Holy Week and finally are almost desperate, finding no ready help. For no one seems to write for the spiritual babes. Writers on prayer have gone on so far that they forget perhaps that the going is hardest when you first begin to go uphill. So it happened that at last I was forced to discover the obvious for myself. Knowing that my own efforts would achieve nothing I turned to our Lord and told him about it. Surely he waits for those of us who are weak, to do just this, however crudely : 'O God I never come near you or learn about you and by myself I never shall. Help me in this also, you who have already loved and redeemed me.' Such a prayer will certainly be granted for we have asked Love itself for help. What happens next is entirely individual. Perhaps someone remarks that they like to read through the Gospels very slowly, a verse or two at a time. The spiritual infant may then decide that this at least could be attempted, and if she forgets to read and think during the day, she will accept that failure but at least read before she sleeps; and she may make a direct request to our Lord that he should remind her that she has an appointment with him. Slowly the Holy Spirit breathes upon the grey ashes kindling them; when we read the Gospel we first commend our reading to God; wisely, for so we have turned our hearts a little towards him. If we forget to do this, the Gospel itself reminds us so that we stop and begin again. Our Lord was not choosey about his friends on earth and will not mind our uncouthness if we truly seek him.

It is to be emphasized that what I describe is but a beginning of a very obvious kind; but none of this is nearly so obvious to the person concerned for whom it is light, discovery and direction. Now at last we know that God is there always, closer than breathing, nearer than sight, not minding our muddles. There is wordless prayer, our own Book of Common Prayer has endless treasure and all usages are open to us; yet at first perhaps we do well to stumble into our own words for only so do our thoughts gain meaning and purpose. ('How can I know what I think till I see what I say?') If we ask for help, if we say we are sorry, we do so in plain terms. Perhaps we record the names of people for whom we pray in a cheap notebook; we get a Bible with references and begin to try to fill in the background. It is of course difficult and unwise to tackle the whole of Scripture unaided; but the Gospels have power to nourish even without the help of notes. First comes the gospel, then a desire to understand, then, in some degree, study. *To begin* with the notes can kill thought and imagination—or so I have found.

In fact we begin to do what we ought to have been doing for years, but we do not worry about the fact since we can be certain that it does not worry our Lord. In time we may catch up with the manuals of prayer and begin at their beginning. While we learn these things, the sacrament of Holy Communion gains fresh meaning. We use it not because we feel like doing so but because we have been told to do so. 'Do this, in remembrance of me. Never mind your sleepiness, your wandering thoughts, your fidgetting children. Do this.' The Church has betrayed and denied her Lord again and again; this one order at least she has obeyed.

It could be said that the process I have described is unnecessary. What are the clergy and spiritual directors for? One can only reply that one hesitates to bother a busy priest with one's vague inability to pray; and if one does approach him he is usually much too kind and assumes a far greater spiritual knowledge in one than exists in fact. In any case the true turning to God which begins the surrender of our will to his can only be accomplished by each soul, alone. It is a small thing to do, and it will have been done by my will, if I do it, and from my need. Much later I may see that there was also a pattern, that the initiative was both mine and not mine, that the divine patience has been all the time at work, that this small thing was momentous.

7

# THE VALLEY OF THE SHADOW

God cloth'd himself in vile man's flesh, that so
He might be weak enough to suffer woe.

JOHN DONNE

A CERTAIN difficulty arises when one tries to consider an idea
in relation to its everyday setting. For ideas must be put into
words and these come one at a time whereas life is a jumble with
a number of things all going on at once. Thus little has been said
so far of the facts of evil-doing, failure and pain. All of us must
face these facts : they are as relevant for parents as for any one
else. When we are young and if we are prosperous, they weigh
lightly upon us. But at some point we acknowledge that we have
intended good and achieved its opposite ; cruelty, injustice and
folly shriek at us from the papers and the television screen ; pain
and suffering may touch us ; we may even see death that 'can
suddenly make man to know himself.' Our children start life as
innocent bundles : as personality develops it is seen to be flawed.
Our personal failures are a small part of the unhappy whole.

To be aware of some part of this is not new and not in itself
particularly Christian, nor is it for me to repeat what Christians
have said about the situation. The Church contents itself with
the affirmation 'I believe in the forgiveness of sins' and the New
Testament is about reconciliation and the restoring of relationship. Thinking about evil, we can see that it is not a simple
question of people doing the wrong thing when they might have
done the right one. We have learned to see that men and women
and children often behave as they do because they are unhappy
or weak, afraid or insecure. Resentment and fear are among the
most dangerous emotions : their effects are writ large in the

55

world around us. They can govern good people. To put this at
a trivial level; in any close-knit social group one learns quite
soon that to praise A's work to B may be unwise, since it merely
gives B's jealousy an outing. The jealousy may be a consequence
of loneliness, yet it remains jealousy. An unloved child may steal
or bully at school; he is less responsible for this than an adult
would be, yet he has stolen. Peter was frightened and caught off
his guard, nonetheless he denied his Lord. The judicial murder
of Jesus Christ seems to have been rooted in resentment and
fear, but this does not alter its character of murder. To try to
explain is not to excuse or condone, still less does it alter the
facts. But the fears, frustrations and unhappiness that help to
cause so many dreadful things are part of the facts too. These
things have always been understood by those who understand
human nature: since Freud people in general have begun to
enquire why they behave as they do. (Some of the language of
psycho-analysis has passed into common speech, though whether
it is correctly used is another matter.) Not all this is gain perhaps.
We are increasingly vague about right and wrong, though much
in favour of 'happiness.' The blonde in strip cartoons is meant
to be a heroine but she is allowed to lie and to connive at dis-
honesty.

There is too a conflict between what an ordinary person under-
stands of psychology and what a great many Christians (but not,
as we have seen, the Church) have said about sin. There is no
question that a good deal of Christian writing insists on man's
wickedness, on his total responsibility for his wickedness, on his
guilt. I remember listening to an address in Holy Week in which
the following verse [1] was quoted for our spiritual nourishment:
(my italics)

> And make me *feel* it was my sin,
> As though no other sins were there,
> That was to him who bears the world
> A load that he could scarcely bear.

[1] The hymn in which this verse comes has been omitted from the Revised
Edition of *Hymns Ancient and Modern*.

My whole being revolted then, and still does, from this attempt to create in me such feelings of guilt. This attitude is now endemic in Christianity. It does not depend on churchmanship but temperament, and in its varying forms lurks among Catholic and Protestant equally. The revivalist preaches personal sin, personal condemnation and the terrifying baroque crucifixes of Austria have the same message with the Christ a tortured in-human Redeemer-Judge. It is his Virgin Mother who pleads our cause in Heaven. The same attitude is in our Book of Common Prayer. We have only to look at the general confession in our Communion service : 'We acknowledge and bewail our manifold sins and wickedness . . . provoking most justly thy wrath and indignation against us. . . . Have mercy upon, have mercy upon us'—but he *has had mercy upon us.*

There are at least three bad things about this obsession with sin and guilt. In the first place it is a false attitude. One cannot pretend that sin is not real, or that it is ultimately tolerable ; but for Christians to try to see themselves as Caiaphas or Judas is false. (I am not suggesting that it is impossible for Christians to behave like Caiaphas and Judas.) No one can contemplate our Lord's passion unmoved : we do not need to manufacture emotion.

In the second place concentration on guilt removes our attention from God to ourselves and our own sins. Most of us suffer not from infamy but weakness. Scrabbling about in our sins will merely enfeeble us further. Strength and help come from God. 'O taste and see how gracious the Lord is, blessed is the man that putteth his trust in him.'

In the third place, guilt feelings far from helping us to be good will work in the opposite direction, driving us in on ourselves so that we who have nothing to give may try desperately to atone by abasing ourselves :

57

'Self yeast of spirit a dull dough sours. I see
The lost are like this, and their scourge to be
As I am mine, their sweating selves; but worse.'

I believe that psychology does the work of our Lord in teaching
us about the origins and dangers of guilt feelings. As we read the
Gospels we see that Jesus healed minds as well as bodies. Those
who come to him he receives [2]; but guilt does not really believe
this. It is not the same thing as repentance which is the turning
of my will away from myself and towards God. The form of
confession given in the Visitation of the Sick (which is also in
the Book of Common Prayer) is that used in sacramental confession and is splendidly objective.[3] In effect we say: 'Lord I
have done this and this and I am sorry,' and then we pick ourselves up and begin again—which is one of the glories of the
Christian life.

All this is exceedingly relevant for parents. It is horribly easy
to make children feel guilty by magnifying nuisances into sins,
or withholding love. We will tell them frankly that truthfulness
matters, and unkindness is wrong, but we do not deliberately try
to inflict or even encourage the feeling that 'God is good and I
am bad,' for this is to keep them from him. Instead we try to
see that they learn to know that 'God loves me whatever I do.'

We have to admit that Christians seem at times more interested in sin than its cure; they are also accused of glorifying
pain and seeking to suffer it. All of us, sooner or later in this life,
become acquainted with pain in some form, and must come to
terms with it. It is worth trying to think about it a little. There
are so many ways of relieving physical pain that its severer forms
rarely have to be borne by us. It is mostly a useful warning that

[2] Cf. George Herbert's moving poem which begins: 'Love bade me
welcome: yet my soul drew back, Guilty of dust and sin.'
[3] 'I confess to God Almighty, the Father, the Son and the Holy Ghost,
that I have sinned in thought, word and deed, through my own grievous
fault; wherefore I pray God to have mercy upon me. And especially I
have sinned in these ways. . . .'

something is wrong. All the same, when even moderately acute pain invades us it has one overwhelming characteristic: it blots out all other feeling. To respond to other people, to achieve any kind of prayer is for ordinary people at such times a major act of will. It is possible to be detached from, as it were, to listen to the sub-acute pain which many of us meet; it is not possible to do this with acute pain beyond a certain point. In this manner Jesus allowed himself to be invaded, refusing the anodyne offered to him.

It is true that Christians desire to follow Jesus; some of them do inflict austerities, even pain, upon themselves, for his sake. I should not dream of commenting upon what are in effect the private gifts of love; but I am also certain that Christians do not need to feel that they ought to suffer pain. It is not in itself good, therefore not to be sought; and our Lord prayed that it might pass from him. We follow him if we accept the pain which comes unsought and which cannot be removed.

There are non-physical pains which correspond to the physical in being signs that something is wrong: loneliness, fear, frustration, anxiety and many others. As in physical pain, none of these is to be endured without some attempt at a remedy. If God sends us warning he expects us to treat it as such and take appropriate action. If I am depressed or anxious beyond what is reasonable, I will be wise to seek a doctor's help. Other pains, such as disappointment (singularly bitter to taste), do have to be accepted.

Pain, therefore, is not a good; and though it can have its uses, people are in general more improved by happiness than by misery. Yet this is not quite all. It is also true that pain increases knowledge. What form that knowledge takes depends upon the sufferer. To have been ill may cause me to savour renewed health, may extend my sympathies, may teach me that there is more to this world than its surface: alternatively or as well I may have learned to feel ill-used and resentful and perfectly certain that 'no one knows what I suffer.' But whatever the effects on us of pain, we do, at least while they last, perceive life itself in a different way. Pain is not a thing or quality, but a mode of experience.

This is particularly true of a third kind of pain : that occasioned by love. Here come the pains of separation from those we love, until the last parting of all, and the very common pain of having to watch even a mild degree of suffering in someone else. To see our children's friendly overtures impatiently rejected on the playground or at the dancing class; to see them being brave when hurt or philosophic in disappointment is to feel an almost physical pang, for in love we identify ourselves with the beloved. To love at all is to expose oneself to pain, so that true selfishness will very properly avoid such an inconvenience.

The divine love, being perfect in its nature, does not suffer. Pain as we know it is loss, alteration, something spoiled. Thus, although some Christians think that God does suffer, and will tell us that selfishness on our part actually hurts him, I do not see how this can be so. But I can see that our world is so contrary to the nature of divine love that such love is inevitably revealed to us in terms of pain. 'Behold and see, if any sorrow is like unto my sorrow.' This is the great mystery : Christians believe that the Son of God took our mortal flesh and exposed himself to our life. He had no need to do this in order to conquer evil and its results for his own sake, for over him as God they could have no power. But love identifies itself with the beloved and he took our flesh that he 'might be weak enough to suffer woe.' How he achieved the great 'It is finished' we cannot know, but we can see that some part of it lies in acceptance rather than resistance. Having identified himself with man's weakness, our Lord reversed the process by making it possible for man to identify himself with Love. 'If a man loves me, he will keep my word and my Father will love him and we will come to him and make our home with him.' Those who believe in him are to continue his work, loving him, serving him and one another, drawing upon his life for power to do this.

Our Lord's identification with mankind was complete and continuing. Just as man was first made in the image of God, so we are to see Christ in all men. There is no qualification about this at all : 'Inasmuch as ye did it unto one of the least of these my brethren, ye did it unto me.' He is present in the hungry and naked, among those in prison. The face of poverty and crime is his marred visage : the face of selfishness and complacency is his marred by poverty of another kind. The moral condition of my fellow mortal is not my business but God's; I am to relieve his need if I can. Nor are Christians his only friends : 'Lord when did we see thee hungry and feed thee?' We must conclude that if we love our Lord and wish to abide in his love we cannot seek to avoid pain. Indeed he tells us this more than once : 'He who does not take up his cross and follow me is not worthy of me.'

What is this cross? Not for most of us martyrdom, nor even the intended malice of other people. It means the turning of my will to God, the setting aside of my will in favour of his, in religious language, dying to self. Dying is not too strong a word for the effort required to master a quite trivial anger or resentment, or to refrain from excuses. It is not too difficult to rise to a special crisis, but when, for instance, we make an attempt to accept some unkindness (which may itself be imagined on our part) we meet remarkably strong resistance within ourselves. Nor are these angers and resentments trivial in fact: nothing is trivial if it prevents me from doing God's will.

It has to be admitted that the consequences of exposing oneself to divine love can be disconcerting to the observer. Indeed Saint Teresa of Avila roundly declared that our Lord could not expect to have many friends since he used them so ill. Most of us know a number of people whose lives are at God's service; the more this is so the less encouragement of the obvious sort do they seem to receive. I think of Mr. and Mrs. X, with many children and not much money, who exerted themselves on behalf of a family known to them which ran vigorously into debt. The family moved, helped by other friends, and after years of correspondence the local debts were paid at last. One greengrocer was so grateful that he sent Mrs. X a sack of potatoes; since about half of them proved fit to eat she was quite pleased. Again, during the War, Mrs. X made it a custom to take in for the night people who turned up at the police station with nowhere to sleep, and continued to do so long after the worst of the 'blitz' was over. She liked best, one was told, the lorry drivers who made her a regular port of call. Less agreeable were some mildly sinister professional beggars whose bedding had to be stoved, and her most dubious reward was having to give evidence in the Divorce Court after taking in a 'married' couple. Thus, if we are nicely thanked and 'appreciated' and the help we are asked to give is pleasant to give, it is probably because we need a few lollipops to cheer us on. Jesus warns us that when we have done all, we are to regard ourselves as unprofitable servants. There is a reward, of course. The most marked characteristic of the people who abide in the divine love is not their wit, their glamour, or their fashion-value, but their reality. The people who put their own comfort and security first, or who pursue success, or who love power, or to whom social distinction is a necessity look, beside these others, a little unreal, like characters in a novel. The Beatitudes in the Sermon on the Mount are sometimes thought of as an ideal : in fact Jesus is telling us who is happy, or blessed, and, by implication, who is not.

There is therefore no way out of it that I can see. If I want to learn to love, to have true life, then I must begin to put myself at God's disposal; I must begin to die to selfishness and pride. I must embark on an adventure whose end is hidden from me. None of this requires the Stoic courage which I do not possess. God comes to meet us before we have reached him, turning to look for him we find that he is already there. Whatever my *feelings* at any time may be I shall have interior knowledge of what may be called not-aloneness. For some this quickens into more. A young priest was celebrating his first Eucharist. He looked happy, which was natural : it was also as though he had a companion at his side.

The wonder is that we should hesitate.

# 8

# GOD AND OUR CHILDREN

Lear : 'When thou dost ask me blessing, I'll kneel down
And ask of thee forgiveness.'

SHAKESPEARE

REDUCED to its essence, the enquiry I have been making amounts to this : our relationship with our children needs to be a genuinely personal one, and we are unlikely to achieve this unless we have come to terms with ourselves and what we are. The play from which the quotation above is taken shows among other themes just this process. At its beginning Lear regards the world in general and his children in particular as adjuncts to himself. He demands fulsome gratitude from them and flies into a fury when he does not get it. The alteration in him is begun by a complete reversal of fortune which forces him for the first time to consider the nature of the world outside himself, and is completed by the loving forgiveness of his daughter Cordelia. Their relationship restored, and now completely true, is a clear light in the surrounding horror of darkness. Our children 'owe' us nothing, for to 'owe' is a legal concept and love is not law. If we truly love them we need not fear their failing to love us also. What is more, there are few difficulties in dealing with them which will not yield to thought, humour and love's patience. In all this it is of enormous importance for father and mother to mull things over between them. Articles on how to deal with my teenage daughter are entertaining, even helpful, but they can only discuss the subject in general terms. My teenage daughter, if I have one, is not a type : she is a person, and the ideas I may have received must be adapted to her, not the other way round. There seems little point, therefore, in my discussing how one

deals with different children at different ages, even if I were so mad as to think I know all the answers.

There is perhaps more point in discussing the question of our children's religious faith, for here is certainly a concern in which what we believe affects what we do, and in which our basic attitudes are more influential than our professed beliefs. In this department, almost more than in any other, we may feel disposed to ask forgiveness of our children. If I write of it, this is not from any feeling whatever of success (how indeed can one 'successfully' implant religious faith?) but because in the litter of failure some things seem nevertheless important and true.

E

In the first place each family makes its own individual pattern of living, a pattern which depends largely on the temperament of those who make it, and this applies to prayer as to all else. (Are not differences in Christian religious belief to some extent a matter of temperament?) A case in point is Family Prayers. I can see that these are wholly admirable in theory, and that difficulties arising from variations in age can well be surmounted, but it does seem essential that those taking part should not be self-conscious; children and adults alike may find that self-consciousness destroys any feeling of common prayer.[1] I am sure the experiment ought to be made, and equally sure that it ought not to be insisted upon. Grace before meals is another matter and proper to all who believe in a loving Creator. The Jews have a wonderful prayer opening which will apply to almost any situation : 'Blessed art thou Lord God of our fathers who bringest forth fruit from the earth.' Children do enjoy variations in graces and taking turns to say them.

In the second place, although the religious life can be discussed on its own, it should in practice permeate everyday life. I am certain that children learn as much religiously from the ordinary conversation and actions of their parents as they do from the prayers and ideals they are taught. If we are snobbish, if we are careful not to make socially disadvantageous friends, if we are mean to the people whom we employ, if our daily life gives the lie to what we profess to believe, the conflict will not be lost on our children, and they will (unless they dislike us) tend to adopt our basic attitudes. If our behaviour makes it clear that religion is for bedtime and Sundays only, it is our behaviour which the children will tend to learn rather than our religion; but if we recognize, regret and struggle against our failures, this too will have its effect. All that is positive in us will have its influence. Thus children accustomed to living with adults and

[1] I was hopelessly corrupted by a godmother who told me that she used to race frogs during family prayers.

taking part in lively, general conversation are themselves lively and interested. If to their parents the milkman, the baker, the cleaner and the man at the garage are at least potentially interesting people, such they will be to the children. Mrs. Beeton enjoins the housewife not to talk to her servants: what entertainment we should miss if standards had not slipped since her day. 'Humani nihil a me alienum puto' is the humanist's motto. Should it not be the Christian's also?

Another part of daily life is important religiously; the books we read and give our children to read. This is quite as true of non-religious books as of religious ones, and for two reasons. In the first place children, our children anyway, will shy away from direct teaching by their parents on nearly all subjects; and we ourselves hesitate to speak of ideals such as true love, courage, keeping faith, the struggle which is maintained to the last, the life given for another's sake, the protection of the helpless. Still less do we speak of humility and the denial of self. What we can do is to see that our children find these things in the books they read. Fortunately it is almost impossible to write a good book which is enjoyed by children without reference to some of these values.

We need to watch our children's reading for a second complementary reason. Some books written for children are essentially truthful even when the subject is fantasy.[2] They have an internal logic, good can be discerned from bad, to choose rightly is important even when you are East of the Sun and West of the Moon; calamity is possible. Others, particularly for young children, are basically untruthful. They represent a world of talking toys and animals which has no relation to the known facts about animals or toys. Moreover, all difficulties are solved by the equivalent of magical intervention and the atmosphere is

---

[2] There is some excellent natural history in Beatrix Potter, such as the toothless Mr. Jackson, but her animal world is not a cosy one. Some children find it most alarming. Mr. Tod and Samuel Whiskers are genuinely sinister.

an unreal one of excitement and surprises. These books are to the first kind as shop biscuits are to crusty bread and honeycomb. Children can quickly become lazy in mind and if we start them on biscuit books they may find the others hard going. The biscuit books constantly appear as presents, but if we supply and read aloud from the others our children will judge for themselves between the two in time.

I recently had reason to be thankful that our children's school has no time for biscuit books either, and does not teach the children that nature is all pretty birds and daisies. We were in the Welsh hills during the lambing season. The meadow beside us presented the traditional idyll, but a short walk into the hills discovered several pathetic bodies, victims of a bad lambing season or the carrion crows. Our youngest, who three years earlier found the Tale of Mrs. Tittlemouse deeply distressing and is not at all callous now, informed me that this was 'nature.'

If we next think of specifically religious teaching we still cannot keep it in a tidy labelled box; for children have a way of dragging theology into general conversation, demanding an answer to their question. Thus 'Who is God's wife?' is easy although it hardly reflects much credit on Mum's teaching. 'I bet the devil's sweat is poisonous' can safely be ignored. But 'How did Jesus get alive again?' and 'When did Mary really know that Jesus was God's son?' are questions not simple to answer. Yet I believe we must answer, and do so honestly. To be evasive has an effect parallel to evasiveness over questions about sex. It conveys that there is something not quite right about this subject or Mummy would give a straight answer. So I personally would risk heresy every time, but would also try to do some homework.

What do we teach them when the initiative is ours? What do we want them to learn? First and always to love Jesus Christ. To this end we give them pictures as soon as they can understand a picture. We say prayers with them and sing to them from the very first. Prayers at bedtime are the focal point for young children. We want their prayers to grow with them, to be a natural activity. For this spontaneity and variety are surely essential. I myself am not happy about elaborate religious exercises for the young, or the carefully worked out schemes of prayer one sometimes finds. Unless used with great care, books of prayers for children can convey the suggestion that it is the words of the prayer that matter, whereas our desire is the praying heart. Some things are obviously right. We kneel beside our children instead of 'hearing' their prayers. (I once allowed someone to watch us say our prayers together. It is an appalling memory.) We make sure that they learn to give thanks, and we encourage them to bring their own life and ideas into their prayers.

Thus: 'Thank you for the party, and for letting us have some of the cake and not only the grown-ups.'

and 'Please Jesus make all the fireworks go off at once.'
'Please Jesus give the lions a good dinner.'
'Please Jesus have a quiet Sunday afternoon for yourself.'

Quite often children simply do not feel like saying their prayers. (Some take to this activity more easily than others, though to all children, I think, the idea of God as creator and preserver comes naturally.) I have lost my temper on these occasions, a very unrewarding thing to do; it is really better to carry on alone and perhaps to vary the regime. What books one uses depends on individual taste, but we have found that pieces out of the Book of Common Prayer went remarkably well. Children like liturgical language. They use it themselves in many of their traditional games. 'What comes next' loses none of its flavour to their taste for being already known. Thus the introduction to Morning Prayer beginning 'O Lord, open thou our lips' is popular, because there is statement and reply, just as in a singing game. Compline too is full of bed-time treasure. 'Keep me, O Lord, as the apple of an eye' says the parent; with a comfortable wriggle comes the response: 'Hide me under the shadow of thy wings.' Many of the collects can be used: they sink gradually into the mind, there, as I believe, continuing their work.

We teach them the life of our Lord. It is worth getting a good selection of Gospel stories with pictures, and once they can read there is something to be said for leaving the book with them, even if it does not remain in perfect condition: children like to make their own discoveries. Later (godparents have remembered their obligations we hope) they read their own Bibles—particularly relishing the more bloodthirsty passages in the Old Testament.

We take our children to church. What service we take them to depends on our pattern. There is no doubt that the Parish Communion has obvious virtues in that it is a service to which whole families can and do come. But it is not the only pattern and does have some disadvantages. The Canticles such as the Te Deum and the Benedicite are part of our heritage; it would

be sad if our children found them unfamiliar. Again, if there is
to be a procession or a baptism the sermon is the first thing to
be cut out of a parish Communion. This tends to have the result
that the sermon loses importance. Nevertheless it is a service
where action takes place and in which children can feel they

belong. It has the added value that the children present will understand much, but not all.[3] There is no danger of their 'growing out of' the Holy Communion[4]; they *must* grow out of the special children's service.

There is of course the question of disturbance and noise. I believe a major factor in this is the fact that in the Church of England we too often equate religion with solemnity. We forget that a church is God's house, and we have this quite dreadful feeling that because we are there we can no longer behave naturally. So parents try almost to stop being fathers and mothers so that they may be worshippers; mothers particularly are worried in this way; perhaps because women do tend to be over-conscientious. Whatever the cause, the toddler comes to this strange potentially interesting but slightly alarming place. Perhaps his parents have felt it 'disrespectful' to bring soft toys or books or pencils and paper. He is made to 'kneel nicely' and when after five minutes he wriggles or tries to explore the pew a little he gets an anxious frown. Soon he is feeling that he needs attention and love and makes distractions to get them and perhaps his poor mother longs to sit down with him in her lap and cuddle him even though the Creed is in full swing, but she does not like to do so. Inevitably the end is noise. There is no question that while no one minds a happy cooing, continuous noise effectively prevents prayer. There is also no question that really young children can be in church and yet not be a distraction provided that they still feel safe and loved, and provided that the toys which clank and rattle are left at home, and that near-by worshippers are prepared to smile or shut their eyes or look elsewhere if they really mind seeing a child move, however

---

[3] One child made a notable contribution to theology by chanting 'Merry God of merry God.'

[4] It must be admitted that unconfirmed children in their teens may need meatier provision for their intellectual teeth than the Parish Communion can be expected to provide; regular excursions to Matins seem a possible answer.

quietly. Some children genuinely cannot be quiet when very young, and it surely does not matter if they wait a year or two and then try again.

It is true that while children are small their presence in church is a distraction to their parents; there are times when one seems not to have prayed at all, and one becomes so accustomed to concentration in flashes that an occasional early communion without benefit of children is curiously taxing. But if the children can think of it as a proper part of Sunday, if to be there is natural to them, it is great gain. I think of a father telling me how he had discovered that his small son was quite happy during the prayers if he could stand in front of his kneeling father whose arms were about him.

There is too the Church's year. Children like Advent calendars, Christmas cribs, palm crosses, Easter eggs and making Easter gardens. True, these are only trimmings and we do not want them to be pious in the wrong way, or to attach too much importance to outward observances; but children have a great sense of rhythm and occasion, and these 'trimmings' form a satisfying part of the pattern which includes hopscotch and fireworks.[5]

What about the sense of sin, and of awe, the knowledge of evil and of salvation? However we may wish to protect our children from evil and fear, we cannot do it. They will learn a good deal about cruelty at school; we cannot prevent fear. A child may become afraid of a particular book—which has to be banished to the attic; a misunderstood grown-up joke will gnaw away for years; it was a missionary film which made me terri-

[5] Jews, again, understand this extremely well with their feasts such as Tabernacles and Passover and their great Day of Atonement. The Hindu feast of lights, Dewali, is another case in point. Food comes in here too. Thus, if the feasts of the Epiphany and the Ascension include a special meal as well as church, they will be true feasts to a child.

fied of music at night. Some fears parents will be told about, but
not all; we can do nothing to defend our children against
destructive fear except be sure that they know very well that we
love them, and that Jesus also loves them and cares for them
continually.

What do we say of awe, of apartness from God and of all
that is implied by the neat labels 'sin,' 'salvation,' 'grace'? I
myself would not attempt directly to teach these things except in
answer to questions. One cannot teach a state of mind or soul;
it is known by experience or not at all. If we begin to love God
we also begin to learn awe and to discover the difference between
ourselves and him. This kind of knowledge is in his gift, not in
ours, and is his business, not ours. We are there to do our best
but we do not make the souls of our children. It is normally not
long before they prefer to say their prayers in private and our
role becomes one of guidance only. If they have not heard his
voice through us there are others through whom he can speak
to them.

Further, our well meant efforts may do serious harm. We may
mean only to show that God is holy and Other, 'of purer eyes
than to behold iniquity'; we are just as likely to give the impression that he is not truly loving, that he is indeed Other, never
to be satisfied, impossible to please. In fact we may succeed only in
awakening feelings of inadequacy and guilt. We can do this too
not by having high standards, whether moral or intellectual, but
by expecting our children to reach them and being disappointed
when they do not. To feel inadequate is singularly daunting to
a child. It was not a feeling I knew in my own childhood : but
I remember once discussing courtesy with someone who suddenly said : 'You know how I was taught manners? My parents
never told me a thing, but if my manners displeased them they
sent out great waves of disapproval for hours.' The words con-
jured up a childhood as grey as mine had been sunlit. No one,

I am sure, means to bring about such an effect; we can only be sure of avoiding it if we deliberately exercise the 'ministry of encouragement.' Children need to be told they are loved, to be praised, to feel that we are interested, and they are acutely sensitive to our real attitude. As in marriage it is the trivial that betrays the truth. If I offer my child an ice and she chooses vanilla and I do not bother to remember, or if I take the line that it really does not matter, she's lucky to get an ice at all, and anyway strawberry is nicer; in effect I am saying that what is important to her is not important to me. She is 'only' a child and as such inferior to an adult, for few of us behave like this to adults.

When we were in a parish the children and I were invited to tea by one of the families there. I remember the occasion vividly because I caught a glance between the mother and one of her children. It was a look of merry love, utterly enchanting. Young children ask so little of us. They do not demand that we should be socially gifted, or witty or good mimics, or clever in any way. They ask only our supporting love.

Is 'holy fear' then unimportant? Of course not. We cannot be 'over-fellowly' with God; he is not Father Christmas. 'O worship the Lord in the beauty of holiness: let the whole earth stand in awe of him.' Inevitably we desire our children to learn quickly what we perhaps have learned slowly; yet this desire has to be put on one side. We hold our peace that God's voice may be heard, in books, in the psalms, in the Church's prayers; heard in conversation or a sermon, obliquely, casually, heard as he wills, and in his time. Our part is to forgive our children and receive forgiveness from them. They need real forgiveness: 'It's all right, it doesn't matter' is not at all the same thing; for to say this does not restore relationship but puts the offender at a disadvantage. (In fact in adult life it is a common prelude to a first-class row.) Children are most generous to the adult who says

she is sorry she has lost her temper; they are not always quite so
generous to each other and we may have to point out that our
Lord is remarkably firm about the matter.

And what do we say about death? and life after death?
S. Paul connects death and sin: 'Since by sin came death.' I
doubt if our experience tells us this. To have seen death is chiefly
to have seen an overwhelming fact. Yesterday I spoke to one I
loved, to-day before me lies what was my father's body. It is
utterly not he. It is something done with, now not needed. It is
noticeable and puzzling that to many Christians death is the
final calamity, even when there is no question of personal grief.
Their immediate reaction to death is one of solemn distress. A
sermon can include an unguarded remark about 'those of us who
are lucky enough to be alive' which makes nonsense of the
Christian claim that death is the gateway to eternal life. It is
certainly true that as William Temple once said 'Faith is always
most difficult when we need it most,' but the facts themselves are
not too hard for children. They understand that things wear
out, or break. The only dangerous thing is to try to conceal the
facts—I have known this work havoc.

To tell children about heaven is more difficult. I tried once to
do it. 'There is no pain,' I said, 'no unhappiness.' 'Yes, but what
do you have to eat?' they enquired, and I acknowledged defeat.
Far more successful was part of a story given to me as a child.
It tells in imagination how a little girl died and went to heaven;
how S. Peter welcomed her at the gate (his windows were full of
scarlet geraniums); how she was overcome with a tremendous
longing for God; how she dashed through the streets with the
saints greeting her from their windows; how finally she ran into
God's arms and he told her that she was his precious and that
heaven was heaven to him all over again because he had her safe
home. A detail our children liked was our Lady's cupboard
where hungry boys and girls could find an apple or a piece of

gingerbread. Obviously none of this is true any more than 'the gardens and gallant walks' or the rainbow, the beasts and the glassy sea of Revelations are true. What it does is to give a child the notion that heaven is the heart's home in a way that mere assertion can never do. It is far 'truer' than my dreary negatives. It is a way of teaching that is enjoyed by the young and therefore effective. In fact it is our Lord's own way; in this as in all else he is the safe guide.

# 9

## 'HAPPY FAMILIES'

> The corn was orient and immortal wheat, which
> never should be reaped, nor was ever sown. I thought
> it had stood from everlasting to everlasting.
>
> THOMAS TRAHERNE

THERE are few parents, however devoted, who will not join
with relish in the 'Goodness how ghastly children are' conversation. Indeed the case against our loved ones is a strong one, for
they are in their nature and from their earliest years dirty, untidy, noisy and egotistic. Even more depressing is the knowledge
that to some extent at least they need to be all these things. If
one meets a young child who is consistently clean, quiet and tidy,
and who keeps out of one's way one feels less pleasure than misgiving. This does not alter the fact that dirt and untidiness make
work, and that unceasing noisy demands for attention are hard
on a mother's nervous system or even a father's if his children
'tickle up the tissue of his tender tympanum
With the tootle of the trumpet or the rattle of the drum.'
If parents fall into a muse about the pleasure of their children's
company it is long odds that the children themselves are at
school or in bed.

Yet it is also true that exasperation is merely a surface froth.
The desire for and delight in children is common to mankind.
It is independent of theories of love or religious belief. (People
who have to travel with young children will say that Indians
and Italians, for example, are far more agreeable to travel
among than the British, because they adore children in general
whereas the British can only stomach their own.) The mother

who for the last half hour has felt like knocking her children's heads together will at once spring to their defence if need be, without any consciousness that her feeling about them has altered. There is nothing so clumsy as gear-changing on such an occasion : yet at other times, particularly if we are trying to take in a disagreeable or unfamiliar idea, what happens inside us really is very like a change of gear. I think the mother is unconscious of change because basically there has been no change. Our deepest feelings about our children are constant. They hear us call them little pigs, toads, perishers, imps of darkness (one might make a collection of the abuse hurled by parents at their offspring) and they know that these are the accents of love. Normal family life is a happy thing even though a self-respecting housewife may not admit as much. It is a happiness taken for granted. Lovers exchanging extravagant avowals and promises know each that it is natural that he or she should love, but feel a kind of astonishment at commanding love themselves. In a family, however, where all is well, children and parents love one another without thinking about it. It is in orphanages that the visitor is plied with eager attention, and it is the child under perhaps temporary strain who is specially demonstrative or demanding. Again family happiness is quite remarkably satisfying. This has probably something to do with the fact that a family is not A plus B plus such children as they produce. It is a growing living thing, changing with its members yet essentially unchanged.

Finally, this happiness is daylight happiness. Here are no romantic shadows, soft lights and sweet music, no gently transforming mists : here, however uncertainly, each day sees order asserted over chaos. The family is warmed, fed, clothed and loved and spirits rise because there are meringues or a picnic. A mother does much the same thing each day; it is a determined addict to self pity who feels that she is 'only' cooking, 'only' washing up, 'only' mending when these jobs are as bricks to the final building. Now and again there are moments, perhaps of family nonsense, perhaps as one glances at the young face concentrating upon a toy or some prep., or gazes at the little dynamo abandoned to fathomless sleep, when happiness is like a sound:

> 'Such a sacred, and home-felt delight
> Such sober certainty of waking bliss
> I never heard till now.'

Some women are happiest when dealing with babies. It is true that a downy head nestling against one's throat is irresistible, but for me the time of true enchantment is in the years after children have learned to read for themselves, and are beginning to splash about among adult ideas and skills, beginning to be truly separate people, with minds as hungry as their stomachs, still turning to their parents for comfort but viewing them with singular detachment.[1]

It is right that we should take this most wholesome of human activities for granted, but it does no harm to remember that there are many countries where we could do no such thing. It is not by accident that where there is gross political evil there family life in one way or another suffers attack. Men dwell in every country who, from whatever motive, seek to treat other human beings as less than fully human. Family life is one of their chief enemies. So the everyday business of parenthood is not a private affair after all, certainly it is not unimportant.

I myself would say more. I believe that God made us so that we might discover the true nature of love and that he invented sex and marriage and family life, so that whatever a man might choose to believe, he could not escape from at least the echo of love. To have a family is to enter one of the schools of love.

---

[1] Like the child who said: 'When Daddy doesn't like our conversation his chin looks as if he hadn't shaved.'

I have written of the happiness that mothers and fathers feel. It is often shot through with a kind of grief. Time, which in the period of nappies and teething seems to stand still, doubles and redoubles its speed as our children grow up. To be conscious of our happiness in them is to know that it is slipping past. 'Stop, Stop' our hearts cry out, 'let me look one moment longer.' We long to keep hold, to preserve, although we do not quite know what it is that so continually slips away from us.[2] The poets are mostly not much concerned with children (unless they are writing about themselves) but they know all about relentless time. 'Brightness falls from the air,' they say. 'Beauty vanishes, beauty passes'; and after all it is as well for our children that it should be so. The love which 'binds another to its delight' damages and destroys. Time itself helps us to render to our children the last important service they need of us : that we should let them go. By bringing about visible growth and change time teaches us what we must do. The process begins early and is continuous. The first time my first child goes to the corner shop to buy aniseed balls, alone, or rides to school, alone, it has begun. In time we learn not to ask too many questions, not to see their letters, not to suppose that our children tell us everything. If we are wise, while our children are still so young as to want us around most of the time, we engage in occupations or interests which some-times take us out of the house. Perhaps we start part-time work. Whatever we do, it helps us by preventing us from living on our children and it helps them. They are capable of being greedy about our time with them ; if we allow them to do so, they will grudge us an evening out. That is our own fault if it happens; at heart they are happier if we plainly have our private lives and personal interests however boring or incomprehensible these may be. For so we give them freedom. Subconsciously they know that if Mum really does prefer walking round a smelly sewage farm bird-watching to taking tea with her darlings, then they too can

[2] Children can be a source of sharp physical delight and in them beauty runs in and out of the house. Perhaps it is beauty itself which we so long to keep from vanishing away.

81

be sure I myself am free of it. Knowledge alone is not enough : if it were the human race could long since have enjoyed peace and happiness, and Jesus Christ need not have been born. I tried to say earlier something of what I believe he was and is, and what he came to do. Knowledge of God and love of him need not now be confined to the religious genius, or depend on individual strength of character. It is also true that Jesus Christ is the only child of woman whom it is safe for one to love without reserve and with complete devotion. It is as though God knew that ordinary human nature needs a focus for its love and gave us that focus. Clever people sometimes write as though Socrates and Buddha were of a kind with Christ. I do not deny their greatness. All the same there is nothing, I am certain, in any literature which compares with the Gospels for brevity, authority, and impact, nor any other figure in history who can begin to compare with Jesus Christ as a human being, or approach his power to draw men to him. Any one can love him : clever people, stupid people, the strong, the weak, the sophisticated, the naïve, dustmen, housewives, kings, politicians, greengrocers, dons, children. There is no one who cannot love him except those, if they exist, who will not have love. The word 'love' is used here loosely. The best of us would not claim that they love God; yet there is no other word. It is the only word we have for the movement of my goodwill away from myself and towards some other person.

Perhaps we may now contemplate Happy Families. Certain qualities are common to all of them. We expect, for example, to find high spirits and vigour of mind and body. The family argues and squabbles cheerfully; its members burst in and out of rooms (door slamming is quite a feature of life) and they are much given to nonsense. Some families go so far as to develop a private language. A further characteristic, often to be found, is a love of truth. I do not mean that the family is constantly arguing whether a thing is so or not, or that dictionaries are kept on the dining-room table, but that it is taken for granted that facts are better known and admitted. There is also a truthfulness of conduct as well as of thought. Just as it is far more restful to tell the truth because you do not have to remember exactly what you said, so it is more restful to deal with people who are honest about their preferences and desires. Once my replies are formed solely with the desire to please, or to be 'unselfish' I am on the road to becoming an exhausting devious person whose remarks must be translated mentally by those to whom I speak. Truthfulness can be compatible with courtesy.

Certainly truthful thinking is vital. If once our children develop a taste for finding things out for themselves, if they learn to expect to give evidence for their assertions, to think for themselves they have the key to unending pleasure and interest. Most of us value truth knowing it to be an aspect of love; we often fear it too, not knowing where it may lead us. But there is no fear in love. It is not necessary to be clever for any of this; it is necessary to be ready to use the mind one has, and to be prepared to hear as well as speak the truth. Happy families have a pleasant ruthlessness about them.

One aspect of truth one hardly needs now to mention, and that is truthfulness about sex. It is excellently handled in many books and pamphlets suited to all ages,[3] and I only mention it now because it is too important to go without saying. I think it is quite admirable that girls and boys can now learn how their bodies work without their parents getting into an embarrassed tizzy about it. Any family doctor could write a thesis on the effects of the shock girls used to get when their periods began. If they were prepared for them at all they were probably given the impression that the process was a thoroughly distasteful one, and this impression would be extended to sexual relationships.

[3] The Church of England Moral Welfare Council gives first class advice and help.

84

socially competent people should be so unwilling to share their inheritance with people less rich than they in this respect. I have often read the obituary of some eminent person who obviously had no time for bores and no scruple in being unkind to them. The writer then adds 'he (or she) was a charming and loyal friend' as though this were a virtue to outweigh the rest. Jesus thought nothing of the kind : 'If you love those who love you, what reward have you? Do not even the tax collectors do the same?' Naturally, this attitude of exclusiveness is entirely reasonable in people who do not share Christian values or beliefs. It will not do for Christians for whom there is no human being of whom it cannot be said : 'This is my brother (or sister) for whom Christ died.' As S. John remarks : 'He who does not love his brother whom he has seen, cannot love God whom he has not seen.' Nothing keeps people away from the Christian Church more than the contrast between the love that is proclaimed by it, and the selfish unkindness of some Christians. In this matter we are like a tourist in a foreign land whose ill-manners can in a few days prejudice hundreds of people against the country of which he is a representative. The Christian family therefore is nothing, worse than nothing, unless it draws within it those in need, particularly those in need of love. Our Lord is given good marks from some people because he kept company with people who could now be labelled collaborators and call-girls; his acquaintance included also men who would have known all about expense accounts, men who were intellectuals, men of position who lacked the nerve to visit him openly, and besides these, the ordinary respectable people who dithered and fussed, and bothered about their own importance. He left us his example, and some very clear teaching in the recorded sayings and parables that no one who follows him can expect to exclude any class of person from the will to help and to love. We can think of the story of the Good Samaritan, Dives and Lazarus or the terrible story of the sheep and the goats (animals which in Palestine look much alike). It may be added that the exclusiveness represented here is sometimes seen in individual Christians, but is really not characteristic of Christian families. I can think of numbers of such homes of which it is true that there is no knowing whom you may meet there if you drop in.

This chapter began with the tiresomeness of children, but we may concede that they are splendidly generous with their friendship. It is unnatural for them to think that accent and colour can constitute bars to friendship and even under instruction they can be remarkably slow to learn. The eye of loving detachment may observe that this is partly because children adore an audience (they really do not require entertainment as much as attentiveness) but this is not the whole truth. They bring with them, as it were, news from a far country. Sometimes when we are with them a breath of air from that land touches us bringing an echo of that which is unknown to us and yet our home. From us they receive their necessary daily bread : protection, food, clothing and that which is bread to their hearts and minds, our love. To us, as to all who love them, they bring in their grubby ink-stained hands the living bread, immortal wheat.

5/6/61